Freemasonry and the Germanic Tradition

FREEMASONRY

AND THE

GERMANIC TRADITION

STEPHEN EDRED FLOWERS

Published by
LODESTAR
P.O. Box 16
Bastrop, Texas 78602

www.seekthemystery.com

ACKNOWLEDGMENTS

I would like to acknowledge all the wise-heads who advised me in this project. Thanks go to Ian Read and Michael Starks.

CONTENTS

PREFACE

This is a somewhat unusual book. It is partly a translation of a contribution by Guido von List to the study of Freemasonry, partly a personal memoir, partly a call to action, but most of all it is a basic introductory study of a topic that would really require many volumes to treat completely. The topic is that of the Germanic roots of the Masonic tradition. In this study I do not want to suggest that all of Masonic imagery and symbolism, or that the entirety of Masonic ritual, are simply lifted from ancient Germanic customs. Obviously there have been centuries of intentional efforts to make Masonic customs appear to have their origins in the Holy Land and to be linked to Old Testament themes. However, the facts seem to point simply and directly to a more "home grown" well-spring for the most basic and most original levels of these customs and rituals. These facts were well-known over a hundred years ago, and were discussed in some detail in a book by the American Masonic scholar George Fort in his 1884 book *Early History and Antiquities of Freemasonry*, subtitled *As Connected with Ancient Norse Guilds, and the Oriental and Mediæval Building Fraternities.*

Our little book begins with a personal memoir that details my own brush with the Masonic Order and how it ended badly, but predictably. This is followed by the main body of the work consisting of two chapters. The first details the historical aspects of the question while the next delves more into specific themes of myth and ritual which have definite Germanic roots. Appended to this is an article written in 1910 by Guido von List, which touches on the Germanic origin of Masonic symbolism. The book concludes with a call to action for all men possessed of the idea of *tradition* to make the effort to become a Mason and thereby revivify this dying institution.

Stephen Edred Flowers
Woodharrow

My Masonic (Mis-)Adventure

Background

In order to understand my exploration of the Masonic Order one must have some background. It did not come lightly, nor did it come without my eyes being open to its eventual outcome. The events are both instructive and amusing.

One of the several things I knew about my grandfather, that grandfather I never met because he died some eight years before I was born, was that he was a Mason. His name was Edred and I was named after him. In my subsequent explorations of the esoteric, the fact that my grandfather had been a Mason — as well as a Knight of the KKK, as the robes found in a chest after his death demonstrated — loomed in the background of my own search for the Mysterious.

Another important figure in my life was Edgar Polomé, the professor who supervised my dissertation, *Runes and Magic*, which made him, in the parlance of German academia, my *Doktorvater*. Several times he discussed with me his involvement with Freemasonry in his native Belgium. In one of these discussions he revealed to me that in the teachings of his lodge, the Master Mason degree and the legend of Hiram Abifff were interpreted in Light of the Myth of the Germanic God Baldur. He also made it known that his own religious personal view was most characterized by a search for the Light. These words would also guide me in the future.

In general I avoided involvement with Masonry because I had come to understand that it was largely devoid of any real teaching anymore, and that its members were largely conservative Christians with little Understanding of what it was they were doing. At the same time I was fully aware from early on that Freemasonic ritual and structure were largely based on old guild customs and organizational principles. This is why I did some research in the late 1970s which acted as a basis for certain features of the ritual and structure of the Rune-Gild.

My Wewelsburg Working, October 2005

In October of 2005 the Rune-Gild held a World Gild-Moot in Schleswig, Germany. After that gathering was concluded I made a magical pilgrimage to the castle Wewelsburg. I had tried to arrange some sort of "official" formalities with the government authorities now responsible for the castle, infamous for its role as training facility for the

SS.(1) As a part of this official visit, I would symbolically and operatively rebuke the role of Anti-Semitism in the history of the place, thus lending the weight of my own authority to combating this negative aspect of the history of the place. As such, I would have thought that officials interested in diffusing this dark cloud hanging over contemporary German life and society would have welcomed such an pronouncement from someone in my supposed position. However, I was told that officials would only meet with me in Paderborn, well away from the castle, and that any official appearance to the visit would be impossible. I rejected their offer. As a further excuse they gave that there had been a number of "satanic" murders done there in the recent past, and they feared reprisals from the press if they met with me on the grounds of the castle! (These "murders" are the stuff of urban legend.) So I carried on with a more candlestine form of operation. (The rebuking of Anti-Semitism was *not* part of the operation, as this aspect of the operation was contingent upon some form of official sanction for its effectiveness.)

The results of the Wewelsburg Working were these: 1) That the ground-space at Woodharrow should be turned into an "instrument of initiation," a school for self-development, and 2) a linkage should be made to a *tradition*. These two results were separate and distinct on one level, but somehow bound on another. The second part led me to conclude that it was perhaps Freemasonry that was intended. Why? It was something which was linked to my own background, culturally and genetically, as well as being a part of the initiation of one of my own major initiators. It was a genuine, if moribund tradition. In some way too, perhaps a living linkage could be made back to the forms which first informed the structures of the ancient gild of rune-masters.

Omens and Good Rede

Before I proceeded to make contact with the Masonic Order in my own local area, I sought out corroborating omens and hail-signs. The oracle of the sixteen runes used in conjunction with the Hávamál definitely warned against the undertaking as a dead-end. The Old Man has, however, been in the habit of testing me in some of these avenues, so I persevered. I also sought the rede (advice) of wise-heads, both of whom were known by me to be Masons of high degree. One told me to forge ahead, as there was nothing in the traditions of Masonry that which disqualify me. There are, of course, many customs in present-day Masonry which an Odian might find objectionable, e.g. swearing on a Bible. But at the same time, I, as a historian of the craft, knew that these were only latter-day symbols for something which I understood to be much older and true. The other wise-head warned me that Masons now generally represent the most conservative element one will find in any given community, and that I should take his into account as I dealt with the Masons in general.

Approaching the Order

As I knew a local Mason, an elderly man who had worked for us when we moved to Woodharrow in 1993, I inquired of him as to how to approach the Lodge locally. I had given this gentleman one of my books— the translation of Guido von List's *The Secret of the Runes* — as it contains a few references to Masonry. I was invited to visit the lodge to attend the dinner that *preceded* the Loge Work that took place at so-called stated meetings. Such stated meetings occur regularly once a month.

The local lodge is in a newer building in a somewhat remote part of the small town of Smithville, Texas. It is basically a metal building that had been erected in the 1970s. Previously, the Masonic Lodge in town was in the most permanent building on Main Street. As the order had dwindled in financial reserves, it was forced to sell the prominent building and move to a more remote and modest location. It should be noted that the Masonic Order owns lodges in virtually every American town of any size at all—literally thousands of them.

Part of the lodge building was a sort of kitchen-dinning hall space. Contrary to what might have been expected, both the Masonic brothers and their wives shared in this part of the activity. Many of the women were also members of the Order of the Eastern Star, the women's auxiliary organization to the Masons.

Upon meeting this group of Masons, there were perhaps thirty people in all present at the first meeting, one was at once struck by the advanced age of these people. I would say the average age of the people was somewhere in the late 70s. (In the few months I was associated with the lodge two or three of them died.) There were a few members who were closer to my own age, one or two even younger. They seemed to come from all sorts of backgrounds. Conversation was for the most part mundane, with any forays into anything more "spiritual" firmly within the Biblical tradition.

The brothers were most impressed when I produced my grandfather's Masonic monitor from 1922. A monitor is an abbreviated guide to Masonic ritual, easily carried on one's person.

Subsequent to my initial contact an interview process was initiated. Three Masons were to interview me in my home before we could go further. The interview took place in the Hall at Woodharrow where the banner of the Gild is on permanent display. During the interview I explained that I was not a Christian, but rather an Odian. The Masonic brothers there were all in agreement that as long as a Supreme Being was acknowledged, in my case Odin and or the Germanic gods, all was in order.

Initiation

An Entered Apprentice rite was scheduled for me on June 21, 2006. The rite was conducted, and a general impression of its contents can be gained from *Duncan's Ritual*. It should be noted that every state in the United States and all different countries have slightly different forms of these rituals.

What was remarkable about this experience is what I willed to be remarkable about it. In participating in this ritual, in this ritualized space, I was undergoing the exact same forms of symbolic actions that my grandfather had undergone, or that many previous generations of Masons had undergone for two or more centuries before. In this process I felt that a link had been reestablished between the current Rune-Gild and the roots of the Gild in certain ancient forms shared between the Gild and the rites of Freemasonry.

My Entered Apprentice ritual was attended by a standing room only crowd. It seemed that my reputation as a writer and scholar had preceded me. At the conclusion of my initiation I gave a short talk on tradition. I was struck by the resonant participation in the actions, the movements and the general elements of space in the lodge. My experience resonated over time and space with all those who had undergone them in the past. A link was forged. The Light was seen.

After this experience there began a period of learning for an exam. This exam would cover a good deal of material which had to be memorized, and which could not be written down. I would meet with my instructor, Brother-X, we will call him, about once a week, and this material would be provided orally and repeated verbatim until it was committed to memory.

It was about this time when the new edition of my book on the Fraternitas Saturni was issued by Rûna-Raven. After my extensive discussion and conversations with Brother-X, which included a discussion of pseudo-Masonry, such as the FS and the Golden Dawn, I determined that the text of the FS-book would not be "offensive" to him. In the meeting prior to my giving him the book, and at the meeting when I actually handed it to him, I emphasized, truthfully, that I was not a member of the FS, and that the book is a purely academic study of the order in question.

He looked through the book, and there was a continued brief discussion of its contents. At this meeting, also, we determined that it was about time for my Entered Apprentice test, where I would recite the memorized material we had been working on.

This meeting took place around noon at the lodge. The next day, around 2:00 PM Brother-X called and said that my EA exam was scheduled for the next day. A couple of hours later he called back and left another message saying that the previously scheduled exam had been *canceled*, and that I should call him. We were to meet the following Monday at the lodge, as usual.

I arrived a bit early. When he pulled up, he got out of his car and held out the book to me as if he was trying to feed meat to man-eating tiger. First he said, "Here take, this book, I can't have it around me." It was

14

apparently "bad juju" in his superstition-filled world. He then said that he could no longer teach me, and that *if* I wanted to go on, I would have to see *if* anyone else in the lodge would be agreeable to do so, which he doubted, considering the despicable contents of this book I had written. Clearly he was tyrannically making the decision that I was to be shunned. It seemed that what bothered him most, or what he said bothered him most, were certain "graphic" pictures. (One actually does show a woman's breast, if you use a magnifying glass.) At that point I did lecture him in no uncertain terms concerning the extreme lack of enlightened thinking he demonstrated — he behaved no batter than a superstition-filled savage — hardly the initiatory product of centuries of Freemasonry.

The next day I wrote a letter of resignation to the Worshipful Master.

From my experience with hierarchical groups I knew that none would "come to my defense." Brother-X was a high-ranking member of the lodge; I had not even taken my first degree. It did not matter that he had remained untouched by the meaning of Masonry. That is just the way hierarchical groups work, and the way they must work. Sometimes things get lost, but in the long-run there is no substitute for the utility of hierarchy for such groups. They cannot function without it, and I understand this.

In the final analysis, given my position and notoriety, it was really perhaps only a matter of time before these "most conservative" and often nowadays "Bible-thumping" Masons would have found me out, and I would have been rejected anyway. No one would ever see the irony that these old gentlemen had long since lost the inner meaning of Masonry and that what I represent is far more like what the original free-thinking, adventurous, revolutionary and even radical Masons represented. At this point, as one wise-head said, Masonry represents cultural conservatism. It originally represented transformation and freedom. It fought superstition and tyranny; it did not represent these things in the world.

In the final part of this book I will put out the call for a renewal of Masonry, not just in the old Germanic spirit which first spawned the order, but in the universal sense of the first modern speculative Masons who represented a brotherhood of all worthy men.

---

1 For more on the Wewelsburg and its role in esotericism during the National Socialist regime in Germany, see the book *The Secret King* (Feral House, 2007).

Roots of Masonry
in the Scandinavian Gild System

History

When we begin to approach the history of anything, we have to be sure that we know what it is we even mean by the word "history." It has only been recently that an academic science called history has been developed. To be sure there were pioneers in the kind of history the modern academic admires, e.g. the Greek Herodotus (5th century BCE)—called "The Father of History." History in the academic sense is the gathering of usually *written* or otherwise recorded data, placing it in a chronological order and subjecting the resulting narrative to the analysis of reason. This is not the only kind of history, however. There is also *traditional* history. This is a narrative handed down from generation to generation which perhaps has no basis in hard historical data, but which as come to be believed by generations of people, and has thus greatly shaped those people's lives and their perceptions of who they are.

In postmodern theory, even so-called academic history has been seen to reflect a myth of its own. This myth is rooted in linear and chronological thinking and the reasonable analysis of this chronology has also been seen as a mythic metanarrative of its own.

In the final analysis when dealing with "history," one must take both tradition and rational analysis into account. Most importantly, one must seek out lost traditions, which might have explained historical facts better than traditions which might have been added later under influences distant from the original idea.

Traditional Masonic History

Although there is what must be called traditional history in the lore of Freemasonry, it is far from monolithic. There are various traditions and streams of tradition found in the Freemasonic world. In Mackey's *Revised Encyclopedia of Freemasonry* twelve different possible points of origin for Masonry are delineated. (Vol II, p. 744) The most important "official" or traditional points of origin are connected to King Solomon's Temple and its construction by the archetypal Mason, Hiram Abiff. The next important impetus comes from the period of the Crusades and the Knights Templar.

The most universal tradition among the Masons is the story of Hiram Abiff, who is seen as the master builder responsible for the construction of Solomon's Temple. Biblical accounts (I Kings and Chronicles II)) mention Hiram of Tyre as a worker in brass and as someone who fitted out not only the Temple but solomon's palace as well with costly ornaments. However, in Masonic lore he is the master builder. He organized the workers to build the Temple and when he refused to give up certain signs of recognition to a group of low-level workers, he was murdered. It is his death and symbolic resurrection which is the myth underlying the Master Mason Ritual.

Solomon's Temple was completed around 953 BCE. This structure was destroyed by the Babylonians in 587 BCE. The Jews, with the help of the Persians, built a new Temple in 515 BCE. This structure was largely dismantled by the Jews themselves under Herod the Great and rebuilt between 7 BCE and 4 CE. Renovations were done to the Temple making it more magnificent and more in line with the esthetics of the Greco-Roman world this third version of the Temple was eventually destroyed by the Romans in 70 CE. On its ruins the Emperor Hadrian built a Temple of Jupiter, which itself fell into ruins. By the time of the Crusades, hardly a trace of it remained.

The original plan of the Temple appears below:

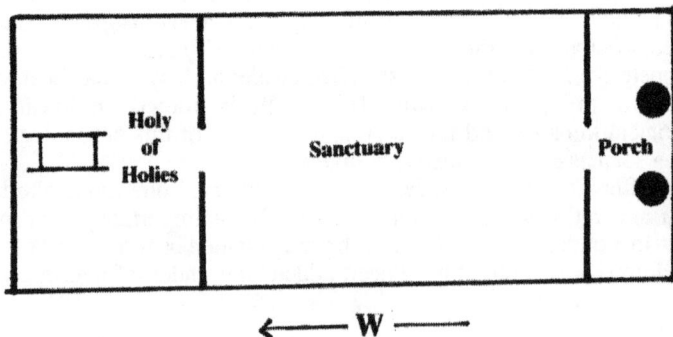

Plan of the Temple of Solomon

18

Another time when the Temple in Jerusalem played an important part in Masonic history was supposedly when, during the Crusades, the Temple ruins were won over once more to Christendom. A German Masonic account presented in the *Signal Star* reads:

> At the time of the [Crusades] under the rule of William II, when Balduin was king of Jerusalem, many noble Scots were persuaded to go along to the Holy Land. They arrived in Jerusalem in 1089, along with the great armies that almost all of Christendom was sending at that time, under the leadership of Robert, the brother of the king of England. They searched to rediscover the holy places, and finally found, after much trouble, four golden salvers stacked on top of one another in the ruins where the holy Temple had stood. In the middle of these salvers they saw the letter J. They immediately recognized the most holy name of the great master Builder of the World, fell down on their knees, praised him and thanked him for this great discovery. As an eternal memorial to this important event they founded the great Royal Order of Scottish Masonry and called themselves Knights of the Temple of Jerusalem in memorial, because the builders of the second Temple at the time of Zorobabel had to carry weapons in one hand and in the other their building tools, because their enemies were always trying to disrupt their work.

Here we see the legendary roots not only of the Templars and their supposed Masonic connections, but also of the Scottish Rite.

Traditionally Masonry traces its roots back to Hiram Abiff and to the builders of the Temple of Solomon. However, even Masonic historians agree that the connections between that time and place and modern Masonry are tenuous. Hiram Abiff appears to be one of those figures supplied from biblical accounts to explain and illustrate in legendary fashion what was being enacted in the age-old gild rituals. Although modern Masonry traces its lineage to the reforms undertaken in England in 1717, the figure of Hiram Abifff does not appear until a short time later in the *Old Charges* of 1725-1730 (Mackey's Encyclopedia, Supplement p. 1259))

Academic History

By way of example as to how traditional history and academic history can be brought together under certain conditions, let us look at the various myths on the origin of the English people. One has it that Germanic chieftains, Hengest and Horsa were invited by the British to restore order to the lawless world of post-Roman Britain. Another has it that they are a "lost tribe of Israel"— the Isaac's-sons = Saxons (!). While yet another holds that they are descendants of a wandering Trojan. The three traditions are, however, not equal in value. The first has ample archeological evidence to support is broad outline, if not its details. The other two are born of medieval agendas and must be relegated to pure myth.

In this section, as I take on the academic history of Freemasonry, I want to show how historical facts (independent of Masonic tradition) must be used to corroborate the story. In the end, however, I realize that many will argue that the version of history I am presenting is just as fantastic as some of the others. I only ask the reader to consider the whole of history, and to realize, as always that the truest answers are usually found close to home, and not in some exotic locale.

To aid in keeping historical events in chronological order — a feat with which many "new agers" seem to have a profound problem — I have included a table of chronological events at the end of the book.

When considering the rational history of Freemasonry, one must keep in mind that we may be dealing with two distinct, albeit related, streams: operative masonry and speculative masonry.

In general operative Masonry can be defined as the craft of building structures in free stone (shaped blocks of stone). However, in a broader sense the craft originally refers to the building of structures in general and goes back to a time before the Germanic peoples were building in stone, to a time when only wooden structures were being erected. Even then there was a builders' gild. In Germany these were (and are) referred to as the *Zimmermänner*— the timber-workers or carpenters. Curiously, the uniform of these workers is that of a long black coat and a very wide-brimmed black hat. That a certain type of "speculative masonry" was being practiced even in the most ancient times when structures were only being built out of wood is revealed by certain Old Norse architectural terminology. For example, the word *áss*, which means on the one hand the main ancient Germanic gods of consciousness, can also refer to "the main beam running along a house," (Cleasby-Vigfusson, p. 46) Beyond this, "the short pillars which support the beams and rafters in a house" are called *dvergar*, "dwarves." (Cleasby-Vigfusson, p. 110) This indicates clearly that pagan theological terminology was used metaphorically in connection with the terminology for architecture. This is a clear indication of the distant roots of speculative Masonry in the North.

George Fort (p. 183) concluded that there were two distinct streams of masonic tradition itself— one a practical one leading back through the Greeks to the orient, and a spiritual one which was at home in the "Gothic" north.

In a sense it is most likely that speculative "masonry" (= constructive crafts) always went along with practical or operative masonry in that ancient craftsmen probably had certain traditions which explained how the worked is constructed and how humanity fits into it which was metaphorically based on the techniques employed in their particular crafts. Builders saw the world as a great structure, cartwrights saw it as a wagon, etc. But in modern times this holistic view becomes less and less common. So, as with so much else, parts of the whole are separated out to fulfill their special functions. Thus practical and technical concerns are excised from philosophical or spiritual outlooks.

Operative Masonry

Operative or practical masonry describes the gilds dedicated to the teaching and preservation of skills of building structures, first in wood then in stone. In a pre-literate world these institutions are indispensable to the continuation of cultural features from one generation to the next. These institutions began in pre-Christian times, but were entirely renovated under the influence of the Catholic Church in the Middle Ages. The Germanic peoples were slowly,a nd often violently, Christianized over a span of about eight hundred years.

Most serious scholars would agree that in the historical Christianization process the earlier prevailing cultural norms of paganism require centuries to be fully extinguished, if they ever can be. James Russell makes an extensive study of this phenomenon for the Germanic world in his seminal work *The Germanization of Early Medieval Christianity*. The ideas contained in his book are, however, by no means isolated. George Fort says:

> It is well known that early Christian missionaries endeavored, so far as practicable, to harmonize the religious observances of Christ and the heathen Teutons. In numerous instances, old Norse customs which alluded directly to Pagan mythology were altered only so far as to furnish a slightly variant objective point, and by this means much that originally represented the fast fading doctrines of the North maintained, under Christian garb, a vigorous vitality. It is fairly inferred that the similarity which presents itself in Frey's ear of corn and Shibboleth, a sheaf of wheat, can be assigned to this policy practiced by early Christian evangelists.

(p. 290)

Freemasons were originally organized as a gild under the Ostrogothic king Theodoric the Great (493–526) in northern Italy— his building program made use of Greek artisans who came to Italy under his patronage. With the fall of the Ostrogoths in northern Italy, the Langobards took over this gild structure. The term freemason was apparently first applied here, The element "free" in the nomenclature alternatively refers to the fact that these craftsmen worked in *free* stone, i.e. cut stone which they worked into shapes suitable for their building purposes, or it may refer to the fact that these craftsmen worked in freedom from royal regulation and restrictions in the time of Theodoric.

The fact that masons were so important to the royal career of Theodoric the Great, king of the Ostrogoths, is perhaps mysteriously encoded in the existence and characteristics of the tomb of that great king. It still stands today in the city of Ravenna, its mysteries still waiting to be unraveled.

21

Tomb of Theodoric

In 726 Leo the Isaurian prohibited imagery to be used in Eastern Orthodox churches. This prohibition lasted 120 years. During this time artisans streamed to the west in order to ply their trade. Many came to Langobardic Italy, where they melded with the builders' gilds originally established under Theodoric. After Charlemagne, the king of the Franks, conquered the Langobards in 774, he undertook the renewal of his own kingdom and empire and as a part of this effort he brought stone masons from Italy to build structures for him in Germany. Many see this as a significant root of masonry in the Germanic world.

There is also a tradition that the Anglo-Saxon king Edwin of Northumbria introduced the craft of masonry in York in 926. This is derived from the fact that Bede reports that Edwin, for his baptism, had himself built a church of wood. Later this was reinforced out of stone.(Bede II:14) Alternatively, this role of being the original mason in England is ascribed to king Athelstan (924-939). But the location of the first English lodge is consistently placed in York. (Fort, p. 114) Ultimately, this identification with Masonry and the northern parts of England is probably a reflection of the deep-seated role Scandinavian practices played in the formation of some of the early forms of gilds in England. The northern and eastern parts of England were under Scandinavian domination from about 886 to 1066. This area was known as the Danelaw.

In the west, masonic gilds were brought under the control of the Church in the early Middle Ages. This was to ensure their Christian loyalty and to see to it that they did not become hotbeds of "pagan resistance." Many monks became operative masons and the lodges were often situated in monasteries. However, around 1200, the governance of the lodges passed out of the hands of the Church. At this time many monks remained affiliated with the masonic gild. Much of the stylization of certain religious figures and ideas in the Church in masonic art can be traced to rivalries within the Church itself. These were rivalries which were reflected in the division between those churchmen who were affiliated with the masons and those who were not.

Since time immemorial among the Indo-European peoples information of a complex spiritual or practical kind has been passed from one generation to the next using a specific *system* of education. This, like so much else the Indo-Europeans created, was arranged in a tripartite way. There were masters, i.e. those who had the special knowledge that others sought. They jealously guarded the secrets of the various crafts— from poetry, to warcraft, to the many handicrafts (e.g. metallurgy, structural building, or wagon-making). These masters, in order to pass the skills along, had to take on young apprentices, students of the craft in question. (Often these could be drawn only from his own family.) In any case part of the economics of such groups is that the skill cannot be too widely taught, otherwise it will be greatly reduced in value. Therefore the Master accepts an apprentice, and he is put to work doing menial tasks, and slowly he is taught various individual skills necessary to the craft. After a certain amount of time has passed, enough skills have been learned and he has been tested as far as his character is concerned, the apprentice graduates to being a fellow. Our English word "fellow" is derived fro the Old Norse word *félagi*, "a fellow." A fellow is one who is provisionally accepted as a colleague. The fellow is sometimes also known as a "journeyman." This word can be taken literally to indicated that the fellow is supposed to journey about the land going from one master's workshop to the next picking up more skills and making himself known more widely in the gild. Once enough time has passed and enough skills have been accumulated and assimilated the fellow will be able to craft an object or perform a skill tantamount to that of a master. He thus creates a masterpiece, which is judged by a group of masters to be worthy of a master and he is subsequently made a master of the gild and thus also becomes responsible to teach other apprentices according to the customs of the gild.

Thus we have a basic three-degree system in all gilds:

    I.   Apprentice
    II. Fellow
    III. Master

Among the warriors of the Middle Ages, the knights of chivalry, these three degrees were: I) page, II) squire and III) knight. This general system remains in effect in European trade unions, and is to some extent still reflected in some parts of American practice. In the academic world this system lies at the root of the three degrees of bachelor, master and doctor. In ancient times, when all free-men might find themselves fighting in battles to defend their tribes, the old gilds often became "militarized." German gilds of the 13th century, no matter what trade they embodied, were always *armed* and went to battle led by their masters. (Fort pp. 203-04)

Because the early gilds guarded secrets of effectiveness, these had to be preserved by men of good character and trustworthiness. This often came down to passing the traditions along only along family lines. (This is reflected in the importance modern Freemasons give to a member's Masonic heritage within his family.) When recruiting outside family lines, gilds often required proof of intelligence and the ownership of property. A gild member had to be a free-man of legitimate birth, that is, no bastard slave or thrall could possibly be a member of such a gild. Such restrictions were also placed upon who could attend the court in ancient times among the Germanic peoples.(Fort p. 271)

The ancient Germanic gilds were invariably dedicated to a certain god or goddess. Some of the gilds were strictly religious affairs, created and maintained for the purpose of performing the seasonal sacrifices and also to provide for the public welfare in times of need.

It has already been implied that operative masonry — the institutional cultivation of technical skills — contains the roots of speculative masonry, i.e. a system of philosophical reflections on life and the meaning of the world based on the system of technical skills.

So what were the building crafts as practiced in the North in ancient times? We know that they built often elaborate and magnificent structures of wood. The Gothic historian Jordanes, quoting Priscus concerning the wooden structures built by the Goths among the men of Attila:

> At no great distance from that place we arrived at the village where King Attila was dwelling,—a village, I say, like a great city, in which we found wooden walls made of smooth-shining boards, whose joints so counterfeited solidity that the union of the boards could scarcely be distinguished by close scrutiny.
>
> (*Getica* XXXIV. 179)

Wooden buildings and ships preserved from the end of the pagan period and from the dawn of the Christianized times give testimony to the sophisticated skills the ancient northmen had when it came to working in wood. The stave churches, preserved for the most part in Norway, provide our greatest insight into the architectural wonders of the ancient North.

Once working in stone was introduced in the North by the Anglo-Saxons and the Franks stone structures began to be built for the first time north of the Alps since the Roman times. At first they imitated the Roman style— in the so-called Romanesque period. But after a while they developed and spread their own style, which later took on the name "Gothic." Just as the ancient Greek temples were really marbleized versions of wooden structures, the Gothic style betrays a spirit born in woodcarving.

Gilds formed to educate craftsmen in the skills of masonry and to act as a sort of trade union for such workers flourished in the Middle ages. But with the dawn of the modern world in the sixteenth century the great secular power of these gilds began to wane.

Speculative Masonry

The use of the rituals and structures of ancient gilds for philosophical (and even political) purposes is what is referred to as "speculative Masonry." The roots of speculative Masonry are essentially three: 1) the inherent and innate philosophical content of the gild rituals, 2) Rosicrucianism, and 3) various occult sciences prevalent in the late 1600s. This book is, of course, exclusively focused on the first of these roots. This is not to say that the other two were not of essential importance to the shape which Masonry took in the wake of the reforms of 1717. Rosicrucianism, besides supplying a good deal of mystical content, also contributed the idea of an international brotherhood of worthy men who would recognize one another as *brothers*, regardless of nationality. It is most likely that it is this idea which most motivated the organizers of modern Freemasonry. On St. John the Baptist's Day, June 24, 1717, four or more old operative lodges of London and Westminster met in London and organized a Grand Lodge. One of the main reasons for the organization was to form a brotherhood — eventually an international brotherhood — of free men dedicated rational thought and spiritual development of its members and to independence from, and if necessary, opposition to the monarchy (tyranny) and the Church (superstition). As such modern Masonry is a child of the Enlightenment. It offered independent free men a mode of organizing in effective ways apart from royal and ecclesiastical authority. As such it became a vessel for the remanifestation of certain very ancient cultural traits which had pre-dated the advent of Christianity and both its rationale for royal authority (divine grace/right) and its own social organization, i.e. the Church.

Modern Masonry is said to have three main tenets, or teachings: Brotherly Love, Relief and Truth. By "Brotherly Love" they mean that the relationship among Masons is akin to that of blood brothers— regardless of the nationality of the brother. By "Relief" they meant to indicate the principle of benevolence and charity. By "Truth" is meant, not only that which satisfies the mind — in the sense that the Freemason seeks to develop his own character and knowledge of Masonry — but also sincerity of conscience and truthfulness in act as well as in speech and thought.

It is true that the reformers of the early eighteenth century could have only partially understood any older philosophical content contained in the ancient gild rituals which they adapted to their own purposes. However, these underlying principles were nevertheless necessarily preserved in the very shape and form of the rituals which they perpetuated. The framers of modern Masonry appear to have consciously sought to "restore" the content of the rituals to their supposed (yet in fact nonexistent) Solomonic origins. To accomplish this they appear to have filled out the rituals with references to biblical lore in those places where they might have been construed to have been suggested. But if we take a more *conservative*, or radically traditional, view we must come to the conclusion that the philosophical content of the rite was more perfectly (if obscurely) housed in the elements of the old gild ceremonies, which can be more naturally traced to the lore of the native inhabitants of England and Scandinavia.

In ancient Germanic times there were gilds dedicated to the sacrificial service of certain gods and goddesses. As the gods often patronized or sponsored certain crafts, e.g. smithing, wagon-making, building crafts, the crafts themselves were also a part of the "worship" of the divinity. In Christian times certain Saints systematically replaced the gods and goddesses, and thus became the "patron saints" of the crafts. These saints were also thought to correspond to the various gods and goddesses and to have taken their places in the lives of the people.

Such gilds were especially strong in early Christian Scandinavia, and this included the Scandinivized parts of Britain (i.e. Scotland and northern England). It is probably no coincidence that modern Masonry emerged from precisely these areas, which accounts for the importance of the York and Scottish Rites. In this region pagan esoteric symbolism was re-encoded in Christian forms and terms. In this way underlying mythic and ritual patterns of behavior inherited from Germanic paganism were retained, but the meanings of these behaviors were necessarily forgotten over time.

In modern times there began an impetus toward speculative or symbolic Masonry. At the beginning those interested in the symbolic aspects of Masonry were entirely ignorant of its deep heritage and its mysteries. They largely accepted the Christianized and Judaized stories and myths woven into Masonic customs. This led them to mistakenly see the mysteries as being "illuminated" by these biblical and pseudo-biblical stories. It would not be until the 19th century and the work of men such as the Brothers Grimm in Germany that the philological and comparative skills would be developed which could more accurately unravel the origins of Masonic customs. However, it must be added that this revelation largely fell on deaf ears, as the masses preferred to believe in the often patently absurd stories rooted in Judeo-Christian imagery. This continues to be so today.

Reflections of Germanic Mythic Tradition in Masonic Ritual

Masonry is now widely held to be a Judeo-Christian phenomenon. Yet formally all that is required to be a member is that one profess a belief in a "supreme being." However, Masonry, as practiced in modern times in largely Christian countries possesses a ritual that has been heavily Christianized over the years. But it is most likely that the ritual goes back to a much simpler pre-Christian archetype which has progressively been masked by conscious and unconscious efforts to make it appear to come from somewhere else.

We are dealing with often undocumented pre-historic events and as such we can never be entirely certain of the accuracy of our conclusions on such matters. Neither can we, in a study of this length, exhaustively discuss all of the ramifications of the ideas in question. However, the overwhelming preponderance of the evidence points to the legitimacy of our interpretation— shared by most objective observers. It is also hoped that this thread of research will be taken up by another intrepid researcher who will being even more light to the subject.

In what follows it is my contention that the major features of original Masonic symbolism and ritual mechanics are ultimately derived from Germanic practices and customs. The fact that this reality is not widely known or believed stems from the fact that the early modern Masons intentionally concealed the basic format under a barrage of Judeo-Christian verbiage. Here we will see many of the features Germanic culture as they gave rise to early gild-based, and ultimately Masonic, symbolism and ritual.

Origins of Masonic Ritual

The complex modern Freemasonic ritual did not spring forth from any one source fully developed and intact. Rather it is the result of centuries of accretion, modification and editorializing. Most of the elements of its rubrics or ritual actions spring from the gild rituals of pre-Christian and early medieval times. The esthetics and much of the ritual verbiage was created around 1700. At that time and subsequently, the speculative Masons had very little knowledge abut the early Germanic roots of their ritual and all their sense of mystery was focused on supposed Old Testament legends which mythically connected their brotherhood to the Temple of Solomon and even to the lore of the Hebrews. Historically there appears to be little that connects Masonic ritual to the religious rites of the Hebrews. As is the case with most things mysterious, the apparent truth is often exotic, but the actual truth is much closer to home.

It appears most likely that Masonic ritual goes directly back to the gild rituals of the late Middle Ages, which were in turn derived from older forms with their ultimate roots in pre-Christian ritualism of northwestern Europe. These rituals were no doubt originally heavily laden with allusions to pagan religion and myth. But Christian missionaries in the north could, of course, not allow pagan "religious" observances to survive— temples were destroyed, priesthoods eradicated, etc. However, the ancient traditional Germanic peoples, like all traditional peoples, possessed a holistic culture. "Religion" was not separate from law, or war, or commerce. Christians saw, and still see religion as a thing set apart from the rest of life. The traditional cultures did not, and do not. But due to this fact of attitude, the Christians did allow the customs associated with what they thought to be "non-religious" customs to continue more or less intact. They did this for practical reasons, for if they had not done so they would not have succeeded as they did. For this reason, gild customs and rituals continued in this manner largely in their pagan forms, as did the rituals surrounding the procedures of the courts of law. Of course, again, where the old gods might have played a role in these rites, they were obligatorily excised in a crude fashion and simply replaced in the formulas by Christian figures. But the basic *structures* often remained largely unaffected.

A gild in the ancient sense is an oath-bound society with some special purpose under the patronage of a spiritual entity. The members contribute (donate) to it, work for and within its purposes, and in turn receive benefits from it— this is the essence of the meaning of the word "gild": It is a mutual *yielding* of various types of resources the individual to the group, the group to the god and the god back to the individual and group. This process was largely effected through certain ceremonial actions and formal interpersonal relationships.

30

We are uncertain as to the exact nature and complexity of the ancient gild rituals. That they existed in some from there can be no doubt. Neither would it be reasonably doubted that these rituals formed the basis of the early Masonic rites. Some gilds were formed in pre-Christian times for the expressed purpose of carrying out (pagan) religious rites. As with the great sacrificial rituals of the Germanic peoples, a festive meal would *follow* the sacrifice. After all the religious sacrifice of the ancient Germanic peoples resembled a "sacred barbecue" in which an animal, manifesting the qualities of a god or goddess, was slaughtered in a manner which ideally caused the victim no fear or pain. The meat was then cooked and consumed by the gathered worshippers, while certain parts of the animal, e.g. the head, forelegs, were ritually deposited in well-shafts, or burned. This attitude toward sacrifice had nothing to do with the Old Testament Jewish customs, which gave the whole animal "to God." (To our own ancestors this would have seemed a superstitious waste.) Repeatedly we hear about how the gilds held banquets after their ceremonial work. Such a banquet was also held after funerals held by the gilds for their members. These rituals often included specific drinking rites which made use of a drinking horn called *Willkommen*, "welcome" in German. Early pre-Christian gilds held these post-sacrificial feasts in honors of the gods and goddesses, as well as their tribal and clanic heroes and ancestors. In Christian times Those so honored could only be God, and the saints of the Church. But still departed family members could be honored as well. (Fort, p. 380)

In Masonic custom, especially in Germany, there is the custom of toasting departed members of the lodge. Since time immemorial in such feasts a garland of flowers, with a rose in the middle, was suspended over the feast-table. This is a symbolic way of indicating that al that transpires there should be held in the strictest secrecy— *sub rosa* (i.e. "under the rose").

The act of ceremonially drinking an intoxicating brew was always a part of the original pagan religious feast. This was an element of ritual which was still observed in the early medieval gild-banquets. Fort (p. 214) describes how the actual ritual of drinking the draught was performed:

> Ancient usage required that this toasting should be performed in three cadences or motions. A glove or handkerchief covered the hand which grasped the bowl; the lid was then raised and finally carrie to the lips and drank in three regularly times #draughts; after which it was replaced on the banqueting table with similar movements.

In connection with what is reported here we cannot fail to notice the three-fold symbolism of the drinking ritual and how it must have originally been connected to the lore fot the three great vats of the sacred mead: Odrœrir, Son and Bodn. All of this symbolism is also probably reflected in the symbol of three interlocked drinking horns found in Viking Age sacred art.

31

Fort (pp. 390-91) notes that in the overtly pagan nature of the gild structure and essence was recognized by clerics in the Middle Ages. They continued to meet once a month on the Calends, i.e. the first of the month according to the newly introduced Roman calendar, and three times a year larger festivals were held. In the medieval period the timing of these was alternatively Christmas, All Saints and St. John's Day (Midsummer), or Christmas, Easter and St. Johns Day. The original purpose of these larger festivals in pagan times was originally religious, legal and commercial. In the Christian Middle Ages the overtly pagan religious component was, of course, lost. However, the rites and customs surrounding the festivals in other areas remained largely the same.

Pagan Court Rituals

George Fort clearly shows that many features of Masonic ritual are derived directly from the practices used in early Germanic courts of law. These courts were sacred affairs in the pre-Christian world, presided over by gods of justice and law. The principal Germanic god of justice is Old Norse Tyr, Old English Tiw. It is from his name that our name for Tuesday is derived, and it is because his day was best suited for legal matters and assembling courts, that early English town-meetings were held on his day. This is also the ultimate explanation for why the American Founding Fathers cited Tuesday as the proper day for elections.

It appears that these arrangements and customs had a significant effect on the form of the Masonic lodge, but that these features were to some extent also influenced by the more religiously oriented spaces used in sacrifice, as well. It is perhaps also possible that these ritualized spaces and arrangements were already synthesized in pre-Christian gild-ritual and that the synthesis of customs is not a later, post-Christianized one.

Courts were called to order at sunrise, and could not go past sunset. Similarly Masonic lodges are symbolically said to open at sunrise and conclude at sunset, the time, it is often explained, when wages of the workers would be received.

Ancient Germanic courts were to be places free of violence and places of peace (Grimm *Deutsche Rechtsaltertümer* p. 745). Many ancient holy places had to be kept free of weapons and metal objects. This was so strictly observed that when in the time of the Christianization, one account tells of how a pagan temple was desecrated simply by having a spear thrown into it. (Bede, II, 13) This perhaps later became the ritualized Masonic idea that to enter the lodge the Apprentice had to divest himself of all metallic objects.

At the beginning of the ancient Germanic court, the judge does the same as the Master of the lodge does in Masonry "by commanding attention and placing the sacred enclosure under the ban of harmony and peace. In this respect the powers incident to a medieval court and congregated Masons may be traced to a custom practiced by the early

Germans, whose priesthood, in such assemblies, enjoined quiet and silence." (Fort, 270) Some of these traits of a Germanic legal assembly are also reported as early as the first century by the Roman ethnographer and historian, Tacitus in his *Germania* (chapter 11).

The arrangement of the court in ancient Germanic times has entirely conditioned how courts are arranged to this day in American courtrooms, for example. In the ancient Germanic arrangement, the judge sat in the west facing toward the east. An altar or other holy object would stand before the judge. To his right, and facing north would be the accused or defendant. To his left and facing south would be the plaintiff.(Grimm II, 432) Other features of the ancient court led Fort to conclude that "In its details a Masonic lodge either directly or indirectly imitated the Norse tribunals."(Fort p. 293)

The entrances into the court-space were more like those found in modern Masonic lodges. Ingress into the sacred space was through one of two openings in the west, to the left and right of the judge.

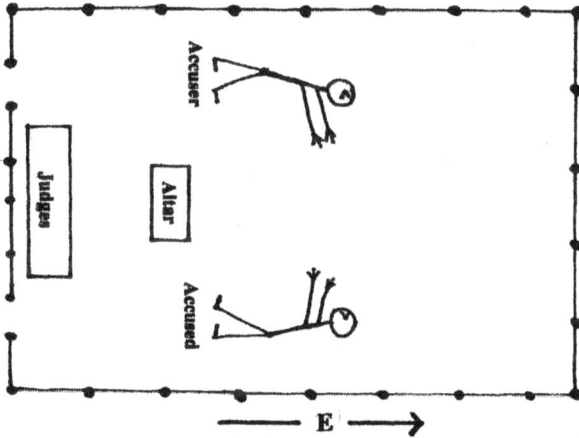

Arrangement of the Ancient Germanic Court-Space

On some matters relating to the origin of important elements in Masonic ritual and custom George Fort appears to be somewhat confused. On page 406 of his study he says:

> Old Teutonic courts were a counterpart of such heathen symbols and ceremonies as the priesthood manipulated in the celebration of religious services. When, therefore, the junction occurred which united Gothic and Jewish elements in Freemasonry,by the merging of Byzantine art corporations into Germanic guilds in Italy, the Norsemen contributed the name and orientation, oaths, dedication of the lodge, opening and closing colloquies. Master's mallet and columns, and the lights and installation ceremonies.

33

Fort goes on to say that It was from a Judaistic source that "Masonry received the #omninfic word, or the faculty of Abrac and ritualism, including the Hiramic legend." That the Hiramic legend as reflected in actual Masonic ritual was in fact not of Judaic/biblical origin, but rather was in fact also rooted in Germanic lore is spoken to on the very next page when he writes: "The traditions of he Northern deity, Baldur, seemingly furnished the substantial foundation for the introduction of the legend of Hiram..." As far as the origins of the "#omnific word" is concerned, that too can be traced to Germanic lore, and will be addressed presently.

Themes in Masonic Ritual

Because of the variegated origins of the whole of Masonic ritual, it may prove to be impossible to reconstruct the archetype of Masonic ritual scientifically. But as a first step we can begin to identify certain themes or elements which have ancient origins and significances.

George Fort provides us with a speculative version of a primitive form of the stone-masons' gild initiation ritual (pp. 212-13) which is worthy of quoting in full here:

> Oftentimes a burlesque initiation was performed upon the applicant, in order to render the genuine mysteries more solemn and impressive. The brethren divested themselves of their implements and short swords in entering the mystic lodge (perhaps in a crypt), for the reason that the highest symbolism of harmony and sanctity was to be impressed upon the suppliant. The lodge being opened in suitable form , the Master presiding directed a brother Mason to prepare the candidate. His weapons, and all substances of like material were taken from him; a portion of his clothing was removed, so as to bare his breast,and with bandaged eyes and left foot unshod he sounded three distinct blows upon the lodge door. Upon his entrance, a Warden received him and conducted him before the Master, who stood in the East. The candidate knelt and a short prayer was offered, after which he was led thrice around the room and back to the door, where, with his feet at a right angle, he was ordered to advance by three upright, measured steps. The candidate was then placed in a position to take the prescribed obligation, which involved contact of his right hand with the sacred Scriptures — holy-dome — and the square and compasses. He swore to be true and loyal, and faithfully adhere o all the charges and regulations of a Mason, and to conceal with care and fidelity the secrets of the fraternity. The bandage was then removed and the three great lights explained. Am apron was presented to him, and having received the password, "Wortzeichen," and grip , "Handschenk," he took his seat as a member of the lodge.

Originally rites of Masonry were concluded with a banquet and certain drinking rituals. Nowadays, at least in America, meals tend to be taken *before* the rites. These drinking rituals often involved a drinking-horn called *Willkomen*— "welcome" in German. Here we are reminded of the images of the ancient Norse *valkyrja* welcoming the fallen warrior into Walhalla by offering him a drinking horn.

Design of the Lodge

Clearly the shape of the lodge and its orientation is not historically based on the Temple of Solomon, but rather on pre-Christian Germanic customs surrounding the arrangement of sacred space. The Temple of Solomon was "oriented" to the *west*, while the Masonic lodge is oriented in the opposite direction, in the same direction as most Germanic sacred spaces were in fact oriented.

Fort (p. 263ff.) clearly shows that the Masonic lodge is based in part on pre-Christian Germanic courts, as we have seen. These environs were in turn based on Germanic religious arrangements. It cannot be discounted that the Masonic lodge of northwestern Europe was also ultimately influenced by the shape and arrangement of the Mithraeum. But that influence would have been only a distant memory by the time of the actual formations of gild-lodges.

It may have been that the original shape of the sacred/court-space was that of a circle or oval— the *Männerring*. This would have especially been so when courts and such affairs were always held outdoors. Tacitus famously comments that "the Germans do not think it in keeping with the divine majesty to confine gods within walls." (*Germania* chapter 9) Perhaps under the influence of buildings constructed ut of right angles, this space was squared off into an rectangle.

Ancient Germanic sacred spaces were conventionally oriented to the east— in order to face the rising sun at dawn. We know from historical accounts and the archeological record that the Temple of Solomon was "oriented" to the *west*. The earliest Christian church buildings were not oriented in any particular direction. It was only after substantial numbers of Germanic people had been Christianized that medieval Catholic churches began to be obligatorily oriented to the east— with the altar in the easternmost direction in the church. This tradition began in the fourth century. (This once strict requirement has in recent years been dispensed with, perhaps due to its known pagan origins.)

The general layout of an ancient Germanic hall or lodge had a fire in the middle of the space, and to the south of the fire was the high-seat (a raised platform) where the king, prince, or owner of the hall would sit. This, no doubt played some role in the arrangement of gild-lodges.

The location of lodges is mythically and metaphorically referred to as being in hills or valleys. Part of the Masonic ritual reads: "ancient brethren formerly met on elevated places and in deep valleys." The idea that masons meet on high hills or down in valleys stems from the historic fact that Germanic pagan temples and places of holding court were conducted in such locations. During the Christianization process churches were in fact often built on these locations. (Fort, p. 198)

Another possible connection with the pagan past lies in the fact that when the great cathedrals were built, the first place the lodge of masons would convene was the crypt— the underground space under the location of the altar. In a practical sense this space provided the necessary concealment of their activities. However, as the archeological record almost always shows, these Christian churches were invariably built on the location, and often even upon the ruins, of a pre-Christian temple or sacred enclosure. The crypt was then in fact the precise location of the sacred space of the pre-Christian site.

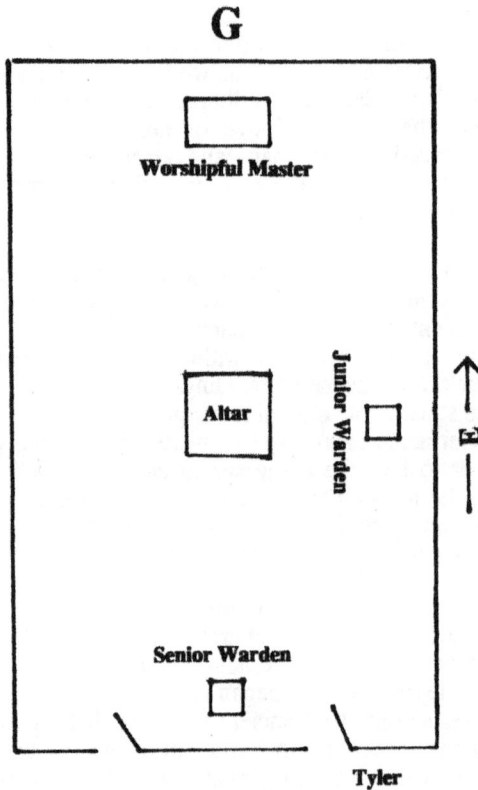

Plan of a Typical Masonic Lodge Room

Masonic ritual refers to the dedication of the lodge to "the holy Sts. John." originally Masonry was exclusively patronized by St. John the Baptist. Only after the 16th century was St. John the Evangelist added. The Germanic symbolism underlying St. John the Baptist is twofold: 1) his

36

particular iconography (the image he conspicuously manifests in art and legend) and 2) the date of his feast day. St. John the Baptist is known for being beheaded, and his head then carried on a symbolic life after being severed. In Germanic lore the god Mímir, whose name means "memory," is beheaded by the Vanir. Subsequently the god Odin preserves the head of Mímir, and it becomes a source of esoteric wisdom for him. The saint's feast-day is Midsummer— one of the three great Germanic festival times, and a time when the victory of the sun over winter is celebrated. St. John's Day — or Midsummer — remains one of the most important secular holidays in Scandinavia today. It remains beloved for reasons similar to those which made it so important in ancient times.

The Three Pillars

In Freemasonry the lodge is said to rest on three pillars of columns: these are named as wisdom, strength and beauty. Fort (pp. 288-89) was of the opinion that these three pillars referred to the qualities of Odin, Thor and Frey respectively. He sites the description of the temple at Uppsala given by Adam of Bremen, as well as the later Icelandic account of a temple in the *Eyrbyggja saga*. Clearly Odin is a god of wisdom and Thor one of strength, while Freyr (as a Vanic deity) could be construed as exemplifying beauty, as did his twin sister, Freyja. These philosophical ideas go even further back, however. The qualities of wisdom, strength and beauty could also refer to virtues of the three Indo-European functions discussed by the French comparativist George Dumézil. For these are indeed the foundations of not only Indo-European myth and theology, but of society as well.

Other obvious and not-so-obvious examples of the tripartite ideology in Masonic ritual include the Three Lights of Masonry. Fort (pp. 290-91) again connects these to the gods Odin, Thor and Frey. He identifies Frey with the sun, Odin with the moon and Thor with the stars. Frey is often associated with light and shining radiance in northern myth, Odin is well-established as a lunar god, but the association between Thor and the stars is more obscure. It is said that the image of Thor is crowned with stars in the temple of Uppsala. Also nails driven (with a hammer, of course) into the beams and pillars of the temple structure were perhaps also seen as symbols of the stars. These are the so-called *reginnaglar*, "nails of the gods," which are depicted in a temple of Thor (*Eyrbyggja saga*, ch. 4). The very idea of "three lights" being important to the symbolism of sacred space is again an Indo-European concept. There were three fires ignited in the sacrifice even in Vedic India.

In Masonic ritual the central altar is approached with three particular steps. Fort (pp. 306-07) speculates that the three steps, indicating youth, manhood and old age, correspond to the three gods Frey, Thor and Odin respectively, which in turn correspond to the three pillars: beauty, strength and wisdom.

The Hammer or Gavel

The hammer or mallet — usually referred to as a gavel — is an important symbol in Masonry. It is also an extremely important one in ancient Germanic myth, religion and custom. It appears to have been inherited both from the symbolism of the hammer of Thor, called Mjöllnir by the Norse, and from the mallet used by judges in early Germanic courts. When ancient Germanic judges opened their courts they did so with three distinct hammer blows. (Again the tripartite ideology is most probably being expressed once more.

In ancient Germanic religion and myth. The Germanic god Thor (Old Norse Thórr, Old English Thûnor) wielded a hammer called Mjöllnir. It was the sacred weapon which kept the giants, forces of disorder and violence, away from the holy enclosure of the gods. It is by the force of this sanctifying hammer that sacred space is governed and protected.

In ancient Germanic legal customs the hammer played no less an important role. A hammer was thrown by a man to determine the extent of the bounds of property he was claiming. A similar hammer-throw was used to determine the size of ground to be used for a sacred enclosure. Auctioneers use a hammer to conclude sales, while judges use one to call the court to order. The power of the hammer ultimately stems from that of Mjöllnir. Possession of a symbolic hammer indicates that the possessor has the power and authority to govern the space consecrated by that hammer. George Fort concluded that the Mason's gavel was ultimately derived from the Hammer of Thor. He notes too that Hiram Abifff was said to have been killed with a blow from a hammer (a "setting maul"). The very word "mason" has been conjectured to come from the word "mace," a sort of war-hammer. However, it is more likely that it comes into Middle English as *machoun* from Norman French *machun*, derived from Old French *masson*, which ultimately stems from Germanic *makôn*, "to make."

The Central Altar

In Christian churches as well as in the Hebrew temple, the altar or holy of holies was in one extreme end of the building designated as the "temple." In Masonry this holiest of places is in the *center* of the lodge. Again this corresponds to the pagan ideal, not the Judeo-Christian one. At the center of the lodge is the Bible. Originally, according to Fort (1884, p. 193), the Masonic book was in that place, which was referred to as the holy-dome (German *Heiligtum*). Upon this book the Masons swore their oaths. The most important of these oaths related to the idea of preserving the Masonic secrets. It is likely that the book replaced the oath-ring on the pre-Christian Germanic altar. It was upon just this ring that oaths were often solemnly sworn.

Typically the central altar in a Masonic lodge is covered with a blue cloth. Fort (p. 295ff.) speculates that this blue color refers to the ancient

Germanic custom of having a "blue" stone as an altar stone upon which oaths were sworn. The *Indiculus Superstitionem et Paganorum* (number 7), refers to oaths being made *super petras,* "over stones."

The central altar and the Bible placed on it is the sacred object for Freemasons. It is called the "great light" of Masonry. One of its chief ritual functions is to act as an object upon which oaths are taken This altar also served this function in ancient Germanic times, although the object upon which the oath was taken was more often a weapon, hammer, ring, or in the case of craftsmen, their tools. The method of Germanic oath-taking mentioned by Fort (p. 315) includes the fact that the oath-taker always faced east with one hand upraised and the other placed on a sacred object. Obviously these liturgical features from ancient Germanic practice continued to be used not only in Masonry, but also in our modern American secular courts.

Various Themes in the Entered Apprentice Rite

Here I will comment on various individual themes or elements found in the Entered Apprentice Rite of Freemasonry. Many of these features form recurring motifs and elements throughout the ritual of Freemasonry, but are first encountered here.

Hood and Noose

No one of English or American heritage can miss the obvious symbolism of the noose and hoodwink that is placed on the person of the entering Apprentice during his induction ceremony. Although these objects and their arrangement are an obvious reference to execution by hanging, i.e. a symbolic death and a certain foreshadowing of the theme of the Master Mason Ritual, it is explained otherwise. Duncan's *Ritual* (p. 48-49) indicates that the hoodwink symbolizes that the candidate was "in darkness" and that he "should keep the whole world in darkness so far as it related to the secrets of Free-Masonry." The noose, referred to as a "cable-tow" is said to simply be an instrument to lead the candidate out of the lodge should he prove somehow unworthy. Execution by the peculiar manner of hanging a person by the neck — especially from trees or specially constructed wooden gallows is a particular mode used by the Germanic peoples— especially when it came to making human sacrifices to the god Odin. In those days human sacrifices were drawn almost exclusively from the ranks of criminals and prisoners of war. The old symbolism referred to both the threat of death by hanging, and to the idea that the candidate was being symbolically killed and reborn when the noose and hood were removed, and the candidate beheld the symbols of initiation.

Hand-Grips

The use of hand-grips as a form of greeting between people is an ancient Indo-European custom. It is first recorded and seen among the

Iranians. In Greco-Persian art we see, for example, the god Mithra greeting king Antiochus with a handshake in a relief from the fifth century BCE sacred complex called Nimrud Dag. This form of physical communication was also well known in the symbolic behavior of the Norse. In Old Norse we have the word *handaband*, "a joining or shaking o hands." This was used in greetings, and as signs of legal contract. It should be noted that Mithra was the god of such contracts in the Persian world, and that he corresponds to the Germanic god Tyr.

"Hail"

The word "hail" (also spelled "hale") is used in the Entered Apprentice Obligation, wherein it says: "I ... promise and swear that I will always hail, ever conceal and never reveal, and of the ... hidden mysteries of Ancient Free Masonry ..." (Duncan, p. 34) "Hail" is an ancient Germanic word meaning "to conceal" or "to hide." In juridical obligations in the German Middle Ages the formula appears *[Ich] will bewahren, helen und halten*: "I will preserve, conceal and keep."

Burial at the Sea-Shore

Another obscure part of the Obligation formula is also illuminated by Germanic lore. It is stated that as one of the punishments for revealing Masonic secrets that the miscreant would have his "body buried in the rough sands of the sea at low water mark, where the tide ebbs and flows twice in twenty-four hours..." (Duncan, p. 34) Fort (p. 319) cites *Frisian Law*, wherein it is stated that if someone broke into and robbed a pagan temple the crime would be punished by "dragging the criminal to the sea-shore and burying the body at a point in the sands where the tide daily ebbed and flowed." Interestingly, Germanic myth indicates that humanity was created by the gods at just this liminal place— the sea shore. (See the *Poetic Edda*, "Völuspá" stanza 17.)

The Twenty-Four Inch Gauge

It is explained that this instrument for measuring length esoterically refers to the idea that as Masons should divide their time into three portions: "a portion the service of God and the relief of a distressed worthy brother, a portion for our usual avocations and a portion for refreshment and sleep." That this idea of dividing one's time into three segments is an ancient Indo-European one is corroborated by the fact that it is mentioned in ancient Zoroastrian scripture where we read that it is one of the duties of a follower of Zarathustra:

> [T]o spend a third of my days and nights in attending the seminary and consulting the wisdom of holy men, to spend a third of my days and nights tilling the soil and in making it fruitful, and to spend the remaining third of my days and nights in eating, rest, and enjoyment.

40

There are many more examples of thematic references to Germanic lore and custom to be found in Masonic rituals. But at this juncture let us move on to two of the most important aspects of this study: the Hiramic Master Mason ritual and the idea of the "lost word."

Master Mason Ritual

The central myth of modern Freemasonry is that of the death of Hiram Abiff, the loss of the "master word" and the three-fold resurrection of the master. The central rite of modern Freemasonry is a dramatic enactment of this myth in which the candidate Master Mason ritually assumes the role of the dead master, Hiram. We know that the Hiram myth, as far as Masonry is concerned, is a modern innovation, with it first being mentioned in a ritual context after about 1725. But if we pay attention to the mechanics of the Master mason ritual far more profound conclusions can be reached. It is most likely that a ritual enactment of the death and resurrection of the Master Mason candidate is based on some older myth, and that some variant of this myth and ritual was used by various gilds in northern Europe and that it is this which became the model for the modern rite.

The Masonic legend of Hiram Abiff may be summarized as follows:

Hiram of Tyre (Lebanon) was the master builder of the Temple of Solomon. When the temple was just about to be finished, fifteen fellow crafts conspired to extort the secrets of the Master Mason from Hiram and travel to other countries to make money using the secret. But twelve of these men recanted from this plot. The other three men not yet qualified to be masters, continued to conspire to force Hiram to provide them with the secrets of a Master Mason, including the Master Word, which only Hiram possessed. These men stationed themselves at the western, southern and eastern gates of the inner courts of the temple. As Hiram tried to leave the temple by the southern gate at high noon after his day's work was done, he was accosted by one of the conspirators, Jubela, who three times demanded the secrets, when Hiram refused, Jubela struck him with a twenty-four inch gauge across his throat. Hiram then attempted to flee through the western gate, and was similarly accosted by Jubelo. Again the demand ws made three times and three times refused. So Jubelo struck the master with a square cross his chest. Then Hiram made his way to the eastern gate and attempted to escape. But the third ruffian, Jubelum likewise demanded and was refused the secrets, whereupon Hiram was struck a death-blow in his forehead with a setting maul. The murderers buried

41

the body of the master in a rubbish pile, and returned at midnight to remove it to a place west of the temple, where they buried it in a grave and planted an acacia plant to mark the spot. Solomon, discovering that the master builder was missing and called the craftsmen together to investigate. The twelve who had recanted of the plot told Solomon about the conspiracy and the king sent them out to search for the culprits. One party discovered the grave and apprehended the murderers, who were summarily executed as oath-breakers. Solomon then ordered the body to be raised and removed from the grave. As the body had been buried for fifteen days it was in a sate of decomposition. Solomon ordered that since the Master Word had been lost upon the death of Hiram, that the first word spoken upon the raising of his body and the first sign made would substitute for the lost ones until the originals could be rediscovered. Hiram's body was then taken to the temple where it was buried near the Holy of Holies.

The Master Mason ritual generally re-enacts these events with the notable addition that when the body is raised out of its gave — the body represented by the new initiate — a hoodwink is removed from his eyes and the one lifting him up (representing Solomon, the Wise) whispers the (substitute) word into his ear. These latter elements, which extend the legend into its ritual purpose, provide the experience of rebirth in a new state of being— as a Master Mason.

In many ways the Master Mason ritual is simply one of the many death and rebirth initiation rites found in many cultures around the world. The main purpose of such rites is to provide the initiate with a *rebirth* in a new form and status in life. Often too there is the reception of a new symbol or teaching. The fact that the initiate possesses this information provides a hidden "certificate" of achievement which, as a "password" allows others who have undergone the same experience to recognize one another, while their identities can remain completely secret as far as outsiders are concerned.

In the history of humanity all initiatory rites, rites of passage, or rites of transformation as they are often called, follow a specific structure. The must first occur a **separation** of the subject (initiate) from his normal or present state of existence, then a **transformation** of the subject takes place while his is in the separate existence, and finally the subject is **reintegrated** into the normal environment, but he now exists in a new form or state of being. In rites of death and resurrection, the subject dies, is transformed while in the realm of the dead and then returned to the world a "new man." this kind of initiation is very common in warrior societies. Part of the function there is to teach the warrior not to fear death.

As the history of Masonry and the history of the myths and legends of the indigenous peoples of northern Europe became increasingly well-known in the nineteenth century many scholars, Masons and non-Masons alike, saw a striking parallel between the Masonic Master Ritual and the myth of the Norse god Baldur. Some were so struck by it that it became the overt underlying myth of the ritual. This myth is recorded in a number of Old Norse poems and the motifs surrounding the myth, or one very close to it, can be found in various artistic pieces from as early as 450 CE. In the nineteenth century the Baldur myth was generally thought of as a "nature-myth"— one about a dying god who represented the powers of nature which "died" in the winter and were reborn in the spring. That such myths exist and are important cannot be denied. However, the Baldur myth is not one of these. The name Baldur refers to bravery and boldness, and the myth is more typical of a warrior rite of passage than it is of a cyclical death and return of the powers of the sun and nature in the cycle of the year.

Here is a brief summary of the myth of Baldur:

Baldur had dreams which foretold od his coming death. His father Odin went to the realm of the dead to discover the roots of these dreams and learns that Loki is planning to have Baldur killed (apparently out of jealousy) but that he will try to use the blind god, Hödr, as his "patsy." Baldur's mother, Frigg, in an effort to make Baldur invulnerable to all possible mishaps tries to exact an oath from every substance in the cosmos not to harm the god. She is successful with all sorts of substances such as metal, rocks, diseases, and so on— only the mistletoe was overlooked because it seemed too insignificant. After this the gods began to play a game with Baldur and hurled all sorts of things at him to attempt to "kill" him, knowing that nothing could really harm him. But Loki discovers the fact that the mistletoe was neglected and fashioned a shaft of the little sprig. He then went to the god Hödr and directs him to shoot the missile at Baldur, who is hit by it and falls dead. This myth of invulnerability is a common one in warrior societies. Frigg sends Hermod to the realm of Hel on Odin's eight-legged steed, Sleipnir, to discover Baldur in Hel to see if he could be raised. There Hermod meets the goddess Hel —Death — herself and she says that if everything in the wold, living and non-living, can be made to weep for Baldur, then he can return. Ambassadors were sent out to try to exact this action on the part of all beings— but one giantess named Thokk (thought to be Loki in disguise) refused to do so— and therefore Baldur remained in Hel. However, in the process of the "judgment of the gods" — the Ragnarök — Baldur is avenged by the god Váli, whom Odin engendered especially for this purpose. It is explicitly stated in the Völuspá that Baldur does return out of Hel after the world

43

has been renewed— will the "hit-man" who killed him, Hödr. In the meantime, Baldur's funeral pyre was prepared by the gods, and before he was placed on it, his father, Odin, leaned down and whispered a secret in his ear.

That this myth was not something created in the Middle Ages is testified to by the fact that the central events of Baldur's killing, or something functionally equivalent to it, is depicted on the Killerup B gold bracteate from around 500 CE— many hundreds of years before the Middle Ages. Here we see the two conspirators and the wounded god, with the mistletoe projectile penetrating his body.

George Fort goes as far as to suggest that Baldur and Hiram are "identical." Fort goes on to describe how Hiram and Baldur can be seen as a "sun gods" and that the story of Hiram and the twelve companions (= the zodiacal signs) and the three ruffians (= the three winter months which killed him) is reflective of this. (Fort p. 408) It is actually doubtful as to whether the myth of Baldur is such a reflection of such natural occurrences. But such interpretations were extremely common in the 19th century. Fort goes on to write:

> Baldur, the second son of Odin, occupies in the Northern mythology, a place similar to Hiram the builder in Masonic tradition. Of so fair aspect and so radiant, he is a synonym of light and beauty. On his life depended the active vitality of the gods of Asgard, as upon the existence of the master architect rested the completion of Solomon's temple— a type of the universe. Baldur was also named the great and

44

good. Hiram and Baldur were equally slain by treachery and fraud. A mallet was the instrument which killed the builder; the mistletoe caused the Northern deity's death. In both catastrophes, sorrow and lamentation prevailed among their associated brethren. A search was instituted to find Baldur, the Norse god, similar to that made for the recovery of Hiram.

(p. 408)

If we look at the structures of the myths involved, we see that there are many similarities. Both figures, Baldur and Hiram possess special powers of abilities which sustain themselves and the world around them. In both cases there is a secret or mystery at the center of the story— the "lost word" and the ultimate secret which Odin whispered into Baldur's ear. Both figures were murdered by a conspiracy. After the killing there is a ordeal undergone by members of their respective societies to recover something, and to try to bring the dead back to life. In both cases the attempts are apparently unsuccessful. However, in both cases also the story becomes the basis for a ritual in which the human enactor of the myth actually is reborn and does receive some secret information which at least points in the direction of the ultimate secret.

One of the chief differences between the Baldur myth and ritual and that of the Masonic ritual based on the legend of Hiram is that the former is a warrior-initiation, while the latter is one for craftsmen. Most of the old pagan lore and ritual was lost, of course. In the case of the Baldur myth we probably only have a fragment of something which was very similar to the kind of ritual and myth used by ancient craftsmen in their gild-initiations.

Evidence clearly shows that the verbiage used in the ritual of Freemasonry is relatively more innovative, while the ritual actions are relatively more conservative. The actions of symbolically killing and resurrecting the initiate is extremely archaic, while the legendary explanation about Hiram Abiff, for example, was instituted in modern times, in the early 1700s.

The Lost Word

The idea of a hidden word, which is "lost," and after which one must seek, is also something of mythic importance in Germanic lore. In fact the myth of the lost and unfathomable word is directly connected to the mysteries of the Death of Baldur. One particular Old Norse poem, the "Vafþrúðnismál" provides a clue. This poem consists of a riddle exchange between an age-old giant, Vafþrúðnir, and a mysterious stranger called Gagnráðr. The giant, because he has lived so long is very deep in the lore of the world and can answer all the riddles put to him. But so too can Gagnráðr. Finally Gagnráðr puts an end to the contest by asking Vafþrúðnir to answer a question that only he knows the answer to:

45

Fjölð ek fór,   fjölðek freistaðak,
fjölð ek reynda regin:
hvat mælti Óðinn,   áðr á bál stigi,
sjálfr í eyra syni?

Much I traveled,   much have I myself put to the test,
   much have I tested the gods:
What did Odin himself whisper, into the ear of his son,
   before he [= Baldur] was placed on the pyre?

Vafþrúðnismál 54

At that point the giant realizes he has been exchanging riddles with
Odin, the god of wisdom himself and must acknowledge that Odin is the
wiser. The point here is that what Odin whispered in Baldur's ear is the
great secret.

The German philologist Franz Rolf Schröder concluded that the word
which Odin spoke in Baldur's ear was *rún(a)*, "secret; mystery." This
word has much to recommend as the solution to this age-old riddle. First,
its etymology relates it to the idea of "whispering," as in the manner of
speech by which secrets are passed. Second, the word would seem to be
the very word first received by Odin in his own great initiation on the tree
of Yggdrasill, after which he conveyed the runes to the world. Third, the
word means "mystery," and therefore is, and remains, an eternal secret
which causes those who hear it to strive for light and revelation
eternally— which is the very function of the "lost word." This word is
the gift given to his son by Odin who abides in the realm of the Dead —
Hel — until the moment of his rebirth in the transformed world of the
future.

46

Origin and Symbolism of Freemasonry
by
Guido von List

Originally published in *Der Scherer* (Vienna) vol. 12, nrs. 17-20 (1910)

If one ignores the obscure, fabulous and legendary history of Freemasonry and merely sticks to the confirmed fact that in the year 1717 the four lodges then existing in London were unified into a single Grand Lodge, which became the Mother Lodge of present-day Freemasonry, and if one considers that these four lodges emerged from operative masonry, then one will have found the cardinal point upon which the question of the actual origin of Freemasonry can be investigated with any certainty. Furthermore, if one considers that the main signs of recognition used by the Freemasons, namely the signs, words and grips (hand-clasps) are not the exclusive property of lodge-brothers, but rather are also known to many gilds, corporations and companies, but most especially and most completely, to the stonemasons, bricklayers and carpenters, who still employ them today. This important circumstance gives considerable indication that the form of Freemasonry stemming from England must only be the renewed appearance of an institution which had previously been known in Germany as well, and this is all the more true because both forms exist to this day in a parallel fashion without mutually influencing one another. This despite the fact that they both possess the same signs of recognition, the same symbols, and in essence similar ceremonial format. If one further considers that the division of Freemasonry into the three degrees of apprentice, fellow and master corresponds to that of practical masonry, and that even the "parlier," (parliamentarian, speaker) made the transition into Freemasonry, and that the most important symbols of Freemasonry are to be found in Romanesque and Gothic cathedrals and secular structures of the earliest period, then the connection with the ancient German constructions — to which reference has often been made — as a matter of compelling necessity cannot be summarily rejected. Many individuals have become known to the author of his present work, who — having belonged to a Freemasonic lodge — knew and demonstrated precisely the

47

signs, words and grips by which they were "taken and accepted in accordance with guild statutes" and upon this occasion acquired the knowledge of these ancient means of recognition, which thoroughly corresponded to those of Freemasonry. The best known and most famous of these individuals was no less than the chief cathedral architect, Baron Friedrich von Schmidt, who died in Vienna on the 23rd of January 1891.

Fig. 1

Since we have identified these signs of recognition, e.g. the so-called throat-sign on the western portal of St. Stephen's Cathedral in Vienna from 1144 (Fig. 1), from the earliest medieval period, where it is carved into stone and comes at the head of a series of mysterious images and declares in graphic form: "I would rather have my throat cut than betray the secret!", the question automatically arises as to what the nature of this secret was, that it has to be so carefully guarded and loyally preserved. Freemasonry likewise refers to its own "Great Secret," which, if they ever possessed it, they have long since lost. This is why it has become a saying that "the secret of Freemasonry is that it possesses no secret." That which Freemasonry guards as a secret, its philosophy, its symbolism, its ritual and its signs of recognition, have been known now for a long time and they are taught and practiced in a much more comprehensive and thorough way in other contexts than in the closed circle of the brotherhood. Moreover, those things which are still regarded as secret are the so-called lodge workings and their other corporate activities— things which every other body also holds secret for obvious reasons. So for a long time these have not deserved the designation as the "Great Secret." — And yet! — *The Great Secret* existed and still exists today. It is concealed in the symbolism of Freemasonry in a "kalic"[1] manner, it is hidden behind riddles and awaits its decoding. To a high degree the Freemasons have earned our thanks because they so well guarded unaltered symbols, rituals and legends which they themselves only half understood, and preserved them unchanged through two whole centuries, as they had received them from the operative masons, who had in turn taken up the legacy from the ancient Germanic carpenters. These carpenters supposedly perished in the turmoil attendant to the Reformation Age.

This "Great Secret" which receives so much emphasis goes back from Freemasonry through operative masonry to the builders' lodges (Strassbourg, Vienna, Cologne, Bern and later Regensburg). The ancient masters had actually concealed this secret in hieroglyphics and secret signs, and this was a secret that was only passed on orally to masters after an exacting test of their characters. This was because it was strictly forbidden to write this secret down or record it in any document. Now understandably further questions arise as to what "Great Secret" the builders' lodge maintained, where its origin is to be found, and finally, the main question, whether this secret can be discovered or understood, or not. It may be said from the beginning that these three questions can be satisfactorily answered.

It is accepted as a matter of certainty that the medieval architectural arts were in the hands of clerics, actually the Benedictine monks, and their lay brothers until the 13th century, and only after that were these skills supposed to be practiced by secular masters, who organized themselves in the manner of a gild and were distinguished according to lodges to which they belonged. These were erected near the sites of great building projects, and thus they called their gild-union a *Bauhütte*— a builder's hut, or lodge. From this it has been erroneously assumed that previously, before there were Benedictines or other clerical architects in Germany, that no stone buildings, or those who knew how to build them, could be shown to have existed in the Germanic countries. However, this is not so. As early as the *Vita santi Severini* by abbot Eugippius (from after 488) several churches in northern Noricum and Upper Pannonia on the Danube from Asturis (Klosterneuberg) to Batavis (Passau) and Juvavio (Salzburg) are mentioned, of which only one is mentioned which was constructed out of wood, while regarding the one only casually mentioned by Cucullis (Kuchel near Salzburg) it is only said that used candles were affixed to the walls of the church. Thus it may be concluded that all the church buildings, with the one exception of Quintanis (Osterhofen), were stone buildings. Additionally, the letter of Pope Gregory I (590-604) to Melittus of Canterbury explicitly speaks of "idolatrous or heathen churches" as being substantial structures, and there are many other artful stone buildings in Austria and Germany, even north of the Danube which were built in pre-Christian times— long before there were any clerical architects. This is proof enough that architecture belonged to the Germans and was not a Roman introduction for which we have to thank the Christian evangelists. Moreover, secular buildings, and therefore secular architects, were obviously necessary.

The merger of clerics, mostly Benedictines, with lay brothers dedicated to the purpose of practicing architecture for the building of churches and monasteries had another cause, however. This was one that was itself the effect of something else, and not the original cause itself. But this cause reaches far back into the dawn of time, into those gray, misty times when after the fall of Imperial Rome, Pontifical Rome was striving to obtain the legacy of the Empire. In doing this Rome sent its first ambassadors deep into the interior of Germany in order to obtain followers for Christianity. The Germanic priesthood, the *Armanen* (Skalds were a subordinate group of *Armanen*) willingly received the apostles and formed mixed colleges with them which introduced the amalgamation of Wuotanism and Christianity as a result of concessions being offered on both sides.

This resulted in the *Kalends*, that is, those who brought about the "change" by means of *kala*, i.e. a twisting or turning (of meanings). Soon, however, they saw themselves as having been tricked and suppressed, but they could no longer free themselves from their bonds. In the Calends, or calendar-brotherhoods, the bishop was always in a leading position, the clerics of the diocese were the leading members, while the laity of the parish had been silenced.*) — At that point the followers of Wuotanism, making use of the two-sided meaning of the word *Kaland* (*kal* = conceal, turn, twist; and = the other, to alter, etc.), gathered together in a secret league within the context of the Kalends2) and likewise with a hidden meaning called themselves the *Kalander*, as they attached the concept of "the hidden others" to these names in a secret [*verkalten*] sense, namely one that indicated "the Wuotanists hiding among apparent Christians." Germanic religion — Armanism as its esoteric aspect and Wuotanism as the exoteric side — was therefore absorbed by those more restricted circles with the *Kalendar***) into the High Secret Tribunal [*Hohe Heimliche Acht*], i.e. something preserved in the strictest secrecy. This secret was indeed a "Great Secret," the care-taking of which was bound up with extreme danger— especially in the late Middle Ages — therefore it need only be remembered at this juncture that this secret was the very suppressed religion of Armanism which was preserved in hieroglyphs that possessed double-meanings. In public these were seen as Christian symbols, but they revealed Armanic and Wuotanistic knowledge in a hidden way to those who knew how to understand them. But since all arts and sciences of the Germanic folk had their roots in, as well as their highest guidance from, the *Armanenschaft* [*Armanen*-institution], the first germination of the of the builders' gild rose up in the *Armanenschaft* itself and the first group of builders were themselves Armanic establishments. According to the nature of the *Armanen*, they moved out throughout the country in small groups led by a master, and temporarily sojourned where there was a building that needed to be built. It is from these wandering construction workers that all the magnificent churches, monasteries, fortresses, and other substantial buildings that we still admire today owe

50

their origins. They were able to unfold the most meaningful artistic constructions in often desolate places with small populations, which is a testament to the fact that such works were the result of migratory artisans, since usually for a sedentary art only the biggest cities offered a suitable place. For this reason too the most important builders' gilds originated in Strassburg, Vienna, Cologne, Bern and later Regensburg and several other cities, while migratory masters of these gilds, along with their journeymen and apprentices, can be shown to have been active throughout the Middle Ages. — It is obvious that it was these very migratory construction workers who occasionally attached themselves for a time to the monks in the monasteries, and thus were often seen as belonging to the monasteries, since, according to the customs of the time having to do with provisions and payment, they would have been regarded as members of the monastic household and treated as such during the time they were engaged in their building activity.

Now since the masters provided for and propagated Armanism, which they had taken into the *High Holy Tribunal* as their *Great Secret* in a secretly haled [= concealed] manner, i.e. their fellows and apprentices were only gradually initiated into these secrets, it was, of course, understandable that they expressed their teachings, which concealed [*verkalte*] or "haled" this secret in certain symbols which were interpreted on three levels, i.e. that they were arranged in three degrees of knowledge in such a way that the apprentice only received the signs of recognition, the fellow received the "Lesser Light" and only the master received the "Greater Light." The apprentice received superficial instructions stated in obscure words; the symbols and words were explained to the fellow in the Christian sense as the "Lesser Light," but only to the master was the "Greater Light" given, and only after he had been tested as being loyal and reliable as an apprentice and fellow did he find out the complete truth about the Greater Light, namely the solution to the concealed riddle, the esoteric doctrine of knowledge in the context of Armanism, along with the responsibility of developing it further.

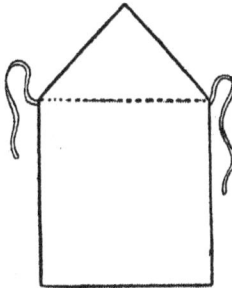

Fig. 2

Gravestone of the Stonecutter and Master Builder Wolfgang Tenc
in the Parish Church at Steyer

Fig. 3

Right from the beginning with the apron, which the apprentice receives upon his reception and acceptance, we meet with the first symbol that tells us a great deal. It has five corners, or actually seven, in that it consists of a square and an equilateral triangle, which appears folded out in Fig. 2. The apron is — contrary to present-day associations — a masculine symbol, while the belt symbolizes the feminine principle. The pentagram is interpreted for the apprentice as pertaining to the five senses. The fellow's apron (Fig. 3) has the triangle folded down so that it appears as being encompassed by the rectangle (square). These Three, Four and Seven were explained to the fellow in terms of the Trinity of God, the four directions according to which a building was laid out and also the four evangelists and the four crowned ones — the four patron saints of the builders' gild***) and the seven Christian virtues, sacraments, etc. Only with the apron of the master (Fig. 4), which is arranged like that of the fellow but lined and framed in blue and set with three blue roses, does the symbolism become clear.

Fig. 4

53

The pentagram, or *Femstern* [five-star], was for ages the symbol of the human-being (the microcosm) as the unification of the five elements: fire, water, air, earth and the aether, which is the same five things being referred to which are concealed [*verkalt*] by the five vowels AEIOU****). At first the apprentice should find these five elements within himself and learn to channel these, i.e. strive to achieve self-mastery before he becomes a fellow. The four gross-material elements form, according to Armanism, the mortal body, the fifth rarified element — *Aether* — forms the immortal soul, which breaks down in turn into the tripartite spirit, spiritual soul and the human soul. As long as the soul remains unrecognized it stands outside the person as it were — just as in the apprentices apron the triangle is outside the square — and only when it becomes aware of itself does its mastery over the body begin and the triangle asserts itself in a dominating fashion within the square. (Fig. 3 and 4)

Only upon this realization is the *ego* (soul, individuality) liberated, in that it subordinates its outer appearances (body, personality) in a conscious and complete way, and thereby completely rules over its body, which is nothing but its mask, and is no longer ruled by the body as it was before. Since this ego [*Ichheit*] is a spark of the divine, a ray of light sent out from the original light (divinity) itself at the beginning of creation ("Let there be light...") — a ray of light that is never extinguished (dies), which at the end of creation returns to the divinity (original light) from which it was projected — every ego (soul) is therefore eternal, without beginning and without end, unborn and immortal, whereas its appearance, its physical personality (mask), is natural and mortal. Every human soul (ego) — as Armanism further deduces — therefore has animated numerous personalities (bodies) since the beginning of time in a long chain of existences and will continue to animate continually renewed personalities connecting each link of the chain one to the other on into the furthest future, from which it can be concluded that each soul, unified with its body — that is, every living person in and of himself — was his own ancestor multiple times over and will also be his own descendent multiple times, until time and space cease to exist. This uninterrupted migration of the human soul, or individuality, from body to body — like a thread upon which pearls are strung — is, however, not to be confused with the so-called transmigration of souls, but rather it is to be evaluated from a much higher perspective. For each individuality shapes its own destiny [*Schicksal*] with respect to future incarnations by means of its own desires, actions or non-actions in the good as well as evil sense. In these incarnations the individual perceives this self-created destiny as happiness or unhappiness, for: "as you sow so shall you reap." The perceptions of happiness or unhappiness in one's present life in a human body are the equivalent of those joys of heaven and the torments of hell which those religions that do not teach reincarnation necessarily project off into the beyond and imagine as lasting for eternity. Now every individual who has penetrated through to such an understanding of his own innermost being must also thereby have gained the conviction that he has to migrate in ever renewed personalities throughout all ages on this earth, and that he, as an integral part of divinity, sought and found this divinity, not outside of himself — but rather within himself — *in the particular spirit of the divine soul.*

This migration of the self within the chain of various personalities through all past and future ages was symbolized by the mystical circumambulations around the square — which the Masons call a tapis — symbolic journeys which the apprentice carries out four times upon his acceptance and reception, the fellow does this five times at his promotion and the master does it seven times upon his elevation.

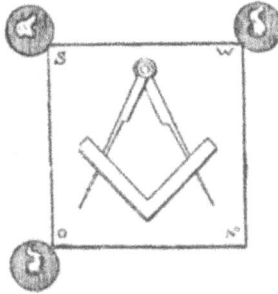

Fig. 5

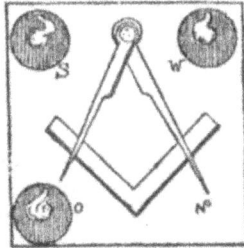

Fig. 6

On this square, also called the *tabula quadrata* (Fig. 5), are situated the "three Great Lights," which in the Apprentices' Lodge are on the outside (Fig. 5), in the Fellows' and Masters' Lodges on the inside, of the square (Fig. 6) at the three corners (east, south and west), while the fourth corner (north), illuminated by no light, lies in darkness. That which was said in connection with the symbolism of the apron with regard to the Three, being either on the inside or outside of the four, is also relevant here. But the connection with the four quarters of heaven, of which three appear illuminated while one remains unilluminated, is a reference to an ancient sun-cult which is also called to mind by the designation of the "three Great Lights" as the almighty architect of all worlds (God), the sun and the moon.*****) And here also the *kala* once more comes into play as the square [*Viereck*] encodes the *Fyroge* (fire- or god's-eye, divine omniscience and human conscience) and "fouring" [*Führung* = leadership]. The *Fyroge* therefore provides "fouring" (leadership) throughout life. Divine consciousness, innate divinity, guides each individual through the gate of birth in the east, into life in a human body, the zenith of which is achieved in the south, in order then to then pass through the portal of death in the west, providing guidance to the individual as it enters the dark realm of death in the north, in order to pass though this place and approach the portal of rebirth in the east. Therefore, Freemasonry today still mystically refers to death as "entering into the eternal east." This is to be understood as meaning that the disembodied individuality of the deceased is on its way to its coming incarnations which occur in the *eternal east* within the Great Portal of Birth, out of which the sun also emerges every day. Therefore the master has to die symbolically at the conclusion of the seventh circumambulation and is placed in a coffin in order to be once more lifted up out of it as a symbolically *reborn* individual. Only as such a person was he then told that he has to seek the "lost master-word" (Armanism) and the "lost unpronounceable name of God" (complete knowledge of the essence of divinity), which he can only find beyond exoteric religious dogmas in esoteric realizations from within his own individuality. Then he is also told that this knowledge, which can only be found on his own intuitively, is not to be given directly to others, because it is not transmittable through words and has to be sought and found by each individual on his own, and therefore it is also called "the unpronounceable name of the divinity."

All the other ancient symbols of Freemasonry repeatedly validate knowledge concerning the foundation and intensification of this main body of knowledge albeit in fragmentary ways. Such symbols can be easily interpreted once one has thoroughly absorbed this main body of knowledge. In this regard architectural symbolism offers a nearly inexhaustible treasury of such hieroglyphic images, from simple line figures to the most richly stylized ornamentation. Here we should refer to the meritorious work of the architect, Professor B. Hanftmann, *Hessische Holzbauten* (Marburg, N. G. Elvert, 1907, 4°) with its many very interesting illustrations. The symbolism of these buildings, entirely in the sense we have outlined in this study, can be seen to go back far into pre-Christian Armanic times.

For our purposes it is sufficient for the most part to clarify the manner in which the concealment [*Verkalung*] took place and that which is essential concerning the Great Secret which the ancient Armanic masters took into the High Holy Tribunal, for to go into the details here is not possible due to considerations of space. Despite the fact that the members' lives were in constant danger, those ancient lodges and their initiated masters preserved and nurtured this Great Secret which the dogmas of the Church so harshly opposed with its unlimited power of control it has in those days. For this reason, and due to the Inquisitional tribunals, such as the witch-trials represented, with their constables who were constantly trying to entrap people, they preserved the Secret throughout manifold persecutions all the way to the end of the Middle Ages. But at the time of the religious upheavals and during the terrors of the Thirty Years War the lodges themselves, along with the Gothic style of architecture, atrophied, and all the initiated masters slowly died out. Esotericism was lost and only its shell, exotericism, was carried forward by half-initiated individuals in misunderstood and mangled forms. But the greater part of the ancient hieroglyphic artworks were preserved down to this day, as were the lodge-rituals and the symbolism of Freemasonry, and because the key itself has finally been found with which to decode these symbols, the Great Secret that Freemasonry so loyally preserved in its closed treasure-house, is now no longer a book of seven seals.

In the eighteenth century, when occult sciences were finding renewed levels of cultivation, such occult ideas penetrated into the lodges of the Freemasons, and since there were many points of concord, the ritual and symbolism of the lodges were influenced in many ways. It was thought that the solution to the riddle and the Great Secret might be found in these occult sciences, which proved to be an erroneous notion, for only in artfully concealed [*verkalte*] Armanism is the key to this solution hidden.

*) *Sachsenspiegel* Book I, Article 2: *EIn ieglicher Christen Mann ist pflichtig den "Senat"* (synod, clerical court) *zu besuchen dreymal im Jahr . . . in dem Bistumb da er gesessen ist . . .* [Every Christian man is duty-bound to attend the "senate" ... in his home bishopric ... three times a year ...]

**) More concerning the Calander, their secret places [*Kalaorte*] and their activities can be found in my writings which appeared in the press of Adolf Bürdecke in Zürich: *Die Religion der Ario-Germanen in ihrer Esoterik und Exoterik* [= *The Religion of the Aryo-Germanic Folk*, Rûna-Raven, 2005] and *Der Übergang vom Wuotanismus zum Christentum.*

***) These are the Saints Servus, Severianus, Carpophorus and Victorinus, who suffered martyrdom on the 8th of November 290 along with five other fellow workers, and who were worshipped as the protective patrons of the stone-masons' gild.

****) The puzzling device of Kaiser Friedrich IV (III) AEIOU was intended to make the five elements subservient o him after the manner of the *Magia mantica*, and therefore constituted a sigil. The usual explanations are therefore invalid.

*****) The sun and moon are polar opposites of the feminine and masculine principles, which the apolar balance of the androgynous divinity transcends; this same interpretation also relates to the three roses on the master's apron. (Fig. 4).

Editor's Notes

1) The word *kala* is one that List seems to have appropriated from Sanskrit. In Sanskrit the word *kalā* literally means "fractions." It is also a technical term for the method of calculating the sixteen permutations of the moon, and of determining the esoteric meanings of syllabic units of sound as they go through similar cyclical permutations.

2) The word *kalends* indicates the first day of the month in the Roman calendar.

Conclusion:
A Charge to All Worthy Brothers

Those who have read and understood the contents of this brief study should feel themselves moved to action by its contents. This can come an inner action or outward action. Different individuals will be called to act differently depending on who they are and what their destinies are. However, I would like to put out the call to action on many reader's parts— a call to reclaim the ancient heritage contained in the outer shell of modern Freemasonry, and to return modern Masonry to its own roots as an offspring of the Enlightenment.

It must also be said that this brief study does not do the subject matter perfect justice. The whole field seems to require a new study on the level that George Fort attempted well over a hundred years ago. His study is sizable, but there is much that has since come to light that would have even further illuminated his discussion.

At present Freemasonry is dying out in America. The average member is in his late seventies— right at the edge of the average life-expectancy. Additionally, the generation which they represent, is a highly *conformist* generation. Whereas the spirit of modern Masonry was a revolutionary, non-conformist one. Whereas the Masons of old were seeking forms of intellectual stimulation — a search for Truth — and a bond of brotherhood which transcended nationality or Church affiliation, the current average Mason is patriotic (in the sense of the "Great Generation") and religiously orthodox. In other words, what started and flourished as a "think tank" for cultural innovation housed in an archaic form of *radical* traditionalism has become a placid pond for cultural conservatism.

There are increasing numbers of esotericists being drawn to Masonry today. This is a good trend. But it must continue and accelerate. (I tried to do my part but failed. I urge those readers who can to make the effort as well.) The Brotherhood is ripe for a major paradigm shift. The old generation is dying out, the younger generation (at present very small in number) is probably dominated by an even more conservative, intolerant mindset than the one it is replacing. But the number of these men is small. Esotericists can make the difference if they willfully act to shift the paradigm of Masonry back to its roots.

Here I am not calling on individuals to turn Freemasonry into a radical traditional schools of Germanic esotericism by returning it to the basic root of the primitive origins of the Masonic rite, which was the subject of the foregoing study. But rather simply to return it to some kind of spirit of esotericism where the system can be used for aims for which it was originally intended. I call on non-Masons to seriously consider approaching the Brotherhood. (The amount of memorization one has to do is about like that of having to take the leading role in a Shakespearean play.) Those readers who are already Masons should take heed of the contents of this book. Masonry will die out completely if it is not made whole. It can only be made whole by returning to its roots, back to its sources, spiritually and intellectually. In a traditional sense it can be the agent for the renewal of the republic and a powerful force for good in our culture. But this is not likely to come about by mimicking what others — church and state — are already doing, and doing badly. The basic values and ideology of modern Enlightenment-based Masonry are the core values of this republic, which have been largely lost. The original spirit of the ancient root of the gilds upon which Masonry was built is the very blueprint of our culture, which has been almost entirely forgotten. Masonry can be the vehicle for the recovery of what has been lost, and for the remembrance of what has been forgotten. It is in this hope that this study has been written.

HISTORICAL CHRONOLOGY

4000 BCE	Indo-European origins
1400 BCE	Zarathustra lives
953 BCE	Completion of the First Temple
587 BCE	Destruction of the First Temple
515 BCE	Construction of the Second Temple
63 BCE	Second Temple Dismantled and Renovated by Herod the Great
70 CE	Herod's Temple Destroyed
136 CE	Emperor Hadrian Constructs a Roman Temple of Jupiter on the Temple Mount
493-526 CE	Theodoric the Great Rules in Northern Italy
638 CE	Muslim Conquest of Jerusalem
768-814 CE	Charlemagne Rules the Franks
ca. 800-1050 CE	Viking Age in Northern Europe
878-1066 CE	The Danelaw Maintained in Northern England
1096	Beginning of the First Crusade
1099	Jerusalem Conquered by European Crusaders
1120	Templar Order Founded
1187	Jerusalem Reconquered by the Muslims under Saladin
1312	Templars Suppressed by French king and the Roman pope
1717	Modern Freemasonry founded in England

BIBLIOGRAPHY

Brentano, Lujo. *History of the Origin and Development of Gilds*. New York: Franklin, [1870].

Duncan, Malcom C. *Masonic Ritual and Monitor*. New York: McKay, 1976, 3rd ed.

Fort, F. George. *Early History and Antiquities of Freemasonry: As Connected with Ancient Norse Guilds, and the Oriental Building Fraternities*. Philadelphia: Bradley, 1884.

Grimm, Jacob. *Deutsche Rechtsaltertümer*. Leipzig: Dieterich, 1899, 4th edition. [First published 1828]

Mackey, Albert G. *Encyclopedia of Freemasonry*. New York: Macoy, Revised and Enlarged, 1946.

Russell, James C. *The Germanization of Early Medieval Christianity*. Oxford: Oxford University Press, 1994.

Smith, Joshua. *English Gilds*. London: Early English Text Society, 1870.

Thorpe, Benjamin. *Northern Mythology: From Pagan Faith to Local Legends*. Ware: Wordsworth Editions, 2001 [1851].

Vries, Jan de. *Altgermanische Religionsgeschichte*. Berlin: de Gruyter, 1956-57, 2 vols.

Wilda, Wilhelm. *Das Gildenwesen des Mittelalters*. Halle: [no publisher], 1831.

www.ingramcontent.com/pod-product-compliance
Lightning Source LLC
Chambersburg PA
CBHW022342280326
41934CB00006B/749